A Gangster's GUIDE To The 10 RULES To This GAME

A Series Of Services

By Terrance Hutson

A Gangster's GUIDE To The 10 Rules To This GAME Copyright© 2021 LinesToLife.Com, LLC
All rights reserved.
No part of this publication may be reproduced, distributed or transmitted in any form or by any means, including photocopying, recording or other electronic or mechanical methods, without the prior written permission of the publisher, except in the case of brief quotation embodied in reviews and certain other non-commercial uses permitted by copyright law.

ISBN: 978-1-7367937-4-9

A Gangster's GUIDE To The 10 RULES To This GAME

A Series Of Services

By Terrance Hutson

Table of Contents

Preface

The 10 Rules — pg. 1

Protect Yoself At All Times/True To You — pg.2-10

Do Unto Others — pg.11-14

Keep Quiet — pg.15-22

Play It How You Say It — pg.23-29

Bomb First — pg.30-34

Each 1, Reach 1, Teach 1 — pg.35-39

Don't Shit Where You Eat — pg.40-43

Anything's Possible. Nothing's Fasho — pg.44-49

Any Is Plenty — pg.50-51

I Am My Brother's Keeper — pg.52-56

A Gangster's GUIDE To The 10 Rules To This GAME

By Terrance Hutson

Preface

This Game has a Bible. I believe in it. And I live the Scriptures. There is an expected compliance in every aspect of living in our society. As children, we were taught to abide by something. And to adhere to certain demands or requests. What was learned, at home, gave, some of us, the preparation for the goings ons in our neighborhoods. The teachings of the neighborhood helped us transition into, damn near, all other settings in life. School? Sports? Streets? Relationships? Job? Where and whatever. When you call on this wisdom, as much as possible, the reward is yours. As loved and loving ones, passing down the practicality of a script is intended to reduce mistakes and drama. It was and is a part of the, protective, character of a caretaker. Your importance to somebody is reflected in the amount of input that person injects into your well-being. Those jewels come with hopeful guidance. Which should never get confused with control. Especially, when coming from a, pretty, pure source.

Some ways to behave are assimilated. Whether absorbed through verbal directives? Visual examples? Or by a, lonesome, trial and error situation? There is, always, a proper way to act. At least, try to 'act' better. Shit. Whether the influences were generic, kind, or hurtful? An, intentional, course of action towards 'your' progress was the, only, motive. Bullshit being picked up from poor ass sources, is a thing. However, being able to put yo finger on the purpose behind these learned traits, should, add to this life, for you. Now to be sure you've received good game, from a good source, ask yourself things like this. Was it worth learning? How do I benefit? Was it programming? What are my rules?

    I have, always, heard that there were ten rules to this game. I thought they might have meant The Ten Commandments. Except, the directives were more realistic for earthlings. Not an unattainable list of feats, only Jesus could pull off. However, I do think the Commandments have a, significant, influence on our 10 rules to this game. I can, also, easily, throw in, some, of the strategic teachings of the 48 Laws of Power. I said, "some" because the book speaks, more to, combat and corporate takeovers, to me. And parts of it, can be used for your, individual, survival. Plus, tons of other literary and visual shares. Or the blending of the collective, tied to how it all fit with our, personal, mannerisms. Which we pull upon, daily. To help us express our commitment to showcasing, solid, human acts.

But who is, the top dog, in charge of setting these rules? Are they getting enforced? And was I supposed to, automatically, know the rules? Right now, and shit? When I, just, found out there are rules? What happens if I don't know? I had questions. I wanted answers. No. Needed answers. Because a lot of mothafuckas was getting knocked down. Behind one somebody's ability to conclude somebody else, "wasn't following the fucking rules." This made it apparent. I was not the only one unaware. Being a kid was my good ass excuse. But older teens and some of the guys in their early twenties, learned the rules to this game on the fly. Winging it. Where slugs, cases, blood stains and scars reminded them of the seriousness of their obedience, to what's law. I got hip, quick, to the psychology tied to the violent examples, set forth.

I associated my take on these, 'hood legal' ordinances, closely, to the rules of the 'dope game'. Or slick street shit. Simply, by the way all the 'real' tough guys, that I knew, appeared to know the edicts of the neighborhood. Shit like, who are the factors, over here? What are the parameters to over here? Who shouldn't be over here and why not? Where I am from, these kinds of questions determine your, own belonging, over here. The answers lead to long lasting life lessons. Gaining the knowledge of who had what and the ticket on them, was privileged info. The type of information, you'd better shut the fuck up about. Then, at the same time, you better seem as if you don't know shit. Plus, you ain't seen shit. Or heard shit. And here, the scandalous ass, teachings were and are still, better than not having a learning, at all.

They would share and teach these customs, with and to the next generation of hustlers. Making other nobodies feel an acceptance. An acceptance into a culture of crime and corruption. That was made for us to lose in life. But succeed in the system. To graduate to a grave. Or you chose, for your own self person, to hop off in the water, with sharks. Joining the school of hard knocks, to study the science of street shit. As a soldier. Or you were hand-picked to play a particular position. Adding to the structure of our chaos. Allocating ranks and duties is a huge part of maintaining and upholding the rules to this game. Keeping gangster ass traditions like, 'standing for something,' alive and kicking. Connecting the why and how for the young, eager, and willing soldiers of the future. Passing down the sense in 'being about it or doing without it'. Giving some direction to the groups of us lost ones, who preferred the darkness. I saw better, there.

Today, however, I apply those same theories to the game of life. As I keep score of life's wins and losses. Living in the promises of ups and downs. And in between our smiles and frowns. Some regulations need to exist. To add to the power in our purposes and choices. From the construction of a set of laws. To the enforcement of abiding by them. The importance of following policies and binding one to them, has been misinterpreted. And therefore, misrepresented by a large part of society. Mostly, consisting of local government and the legal system. It is reflected in their decisions and actions. From improprieties at city hall to the punk police that murdered, Mr. Floyd. I see more violence and selfishness in how they live. They have the faces of hatred. Their voices spew the same disdain held in their eyes. It's these cracka ass crackas. Not all white folks. But who the fuck can tell, these days?

As one Black Man, I deal with more ignorance and disrespect than a, whole, city of whites. Received from the prejudice systems of this country. And one of the few of us, who know where the 'real war' is. I know the 'true' enemy. I know the truth about a patriot, the jew-ish, the irs and this land. The land of my birth. A land, which is now, so politically correct, in speaking, but will, still, operate on the policies of olden times. That do not fucking exist, no more. A country that knows if 'they' would change 3 things in America and America would be cool, finally. Ask me. It's simple. Constitutional and economical evolution. Then, as a union, hold these hoe ass "leaders" to, the same, accountability that a judge will hold me to. I've seen traffic court go harder on regular citizens than the senate or the house. Or congress as a fucking whole has ever. With a 'caught red handed ass,' culprit, still on the crime scene. Make the, necessary, changes and we would have the ability to stand as The "United" states.

To me, knowing what crackas and the punk police are being taught and doing and getting away with, is making fake monsters. But bitch. In me too! Because they are being granted immunity or impunity for these flagrant ass felonies and fouls trespassed against us. This has a lot more of them thinking of themselves as the 'real' "gangsters and thugs" than Black folks could ever consider of ourselves. And for the most part don't, even, see us this way. We, just, found a way to live and love in the trenches of a condition, hatred built. I have more reason(s), "to be afraid for my life," than the 'fake feelings of fear' residing in the minds and hearts of those, scary mothafuckas, trusted with the responsibility of authority. How can't America see that this is A Problem? Why in the fuck not? The answers are exposed in the disregard and disrespect displayed by these 'patriots' towards the elements of truth, righteousness, fairness and justice. This is the criminal and civil fuckery that, exactly, plagues, all, of our, American, lives. While, also, negatively, impacting the shit out of this innocent, family oriented, father, son, brother, entrepreneurial, good, and rebuilt man's life. And fuck you for that.

Is it okay for the law to live lawless? Yeah. I'm asking, as they are, currently, doing it. Yes, I am. Okay. Then, why do I have to give a fuck about the law? Especially, when we all knowing the law don't. Shit! I don't. And to be honest, I never did. Fuck 'em! But I come from where if we set some rules? We are going by them. Everybody! With that. Do you think one set of rules can be applied to any aspect of this life? Why or why not? Or has sticking to 'A' script, let alone 'The' script, become a thing of the past? I believe, most of the 'theories' behind the 'rules' should be applicable to this life. Once I learned to manage the 'how to?' I saw with, pure clarity, what a blessing meant.

I have not been convinced to do otherwise, since.

As this series of services continues, LinesToLife.Com will honor our commitment, to you. We are committed to promoting goodness, self-love, self-awareness, self-respect, class, power, and independence. All the good ways to live and lead your life. We offer a reintroduction or reacquainting to your own, awaiting, spiritual, emotional, and psychological edification. These guides were created to help you focus on finding your best way towards being better. With simplistic perspectives, some deductive reasoning and Google-able evidence to prove our, specific, points. LinesToLife.com wants to be a source of artillery you use when it is time to reload, on the enemy. Or when you feel you are under attack. Resort to your God, which is your guard. Your armor. Then see LinesToLife as the big brother, always, helping you fight. And that we will add insight into the benefits of you being able to make it make sense, to have rules in and to your game.

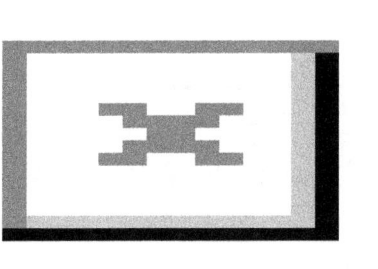

The 10 Rules

1. Protect Yoself At All Times

2. Do Unto Others

3. Keep Quiet

4. Play It How You Say It

5. Bomb First

6. Each 1, Reach 1, Teach 1

7. Do not Shit Where You Eat

8. Anything's Possible. Nothing's Fasho

9. Any Is Plenty

10. I Am My Brother's Keeper

A Gangster's GUIDE To The 10 Rules To This GAME

By Terrance Hutson

Protect YoSelf At All Times

There will be no debating this one. It is the number one rule. Flat out. It, also, carries some important sub-labels attached to its realness. Just as the other rules on this list. Like, 'keep your friends, close and your enemies, closer.' 'If you stay ready, you don't have to get ready.' 'People can only do to you, what you allow them to.' And my all-time favorite, 'love yoself. Because love don't love nobody.' There are more. Shit like, 'don't get caught.' When we stumble up on them. during this guide, let's call them out. Okay? Oh shit! Here's one more, 'if you knew better, you'd do better.' The bullet points and sub-genres to, 'protect yourself at all times,' could go on and on. I will not put us through no shit like that, though. Ultimately, you get the picture. A sense of self-awareness needs to be alive in you. To ensure, you don't feel you must endure, any, time in torture. That time cannot be returned. Which tops the list of reasons I should have said fuck you, in the first place. I mean, with self-preservation being a natural thing and all. And now, I am, also, pissed because I did not go with my first fucking mind. Where in my way of believing, I'd claim that it is my God speaking, directly, to me. Especially, if I am reasoning with myself, aloud.

I don't know if we are, all, feeling like we are under some, kind of regular attack? Maybe we are. By sounding or thinking paranoid as fuck. Regardless. You must protect yourself, at all times. In, choppy, foreign waters. Through the times you find yourself in unfamiliar territory. In, any, scenario. Staying spiritually and mentally sound, is your best defensive stance. Now, this might be obvious, as shit, when reading it. But you know when we are in the middle of the shit. We never believe or don't see there's an out or an end. We can't tell nobody or ask for help. First. Who gone give a fuck? So, why say anything? Then who would understand? What's crazy about that question is, most everybody can understand, what you're going through. Simply because they are going through it, coming out of it or they are about to face it. It, still, doesn't stop us from making it seem like we are the, only, soul something is happening to.

Now, here comes the turtle move, we do. The shell tucks. The scurry back in our holes of pity and fear. Where we'd live in the lie of how much better the isolation is for us. And maybe, this too, is a form of guarding ourselves. But is it helping, though? Or is it knocking us, smooth, off our square? Sending mothafuckas back down a spiral of winding stresses. A stress, brought on by the, only, true enemy that you're fighting. Yo damn self! This action seems natural. But it's not. Believe it or not. We have been conditioned to care less for the 'tribe'. Which allows more selfish room, to think you are alone. We've been made to not understand the importance of knowing 'your tribe'. The benefit of having your tribe is a secret they, intentionally, bury. And have buried. Now that those secrets have been uncovered, here. Find your tribe. Have a reunion. And have the help, assistance, support, and the power, we know we need to make it. All the basics of survival are learned with, around and from your tribe. Your people. I believe, this plan, was and still is, an agenda pushed to keep us missing these pieces to peace.

    Stay mindful of what protection means, to you. How do 'you' define it? The need to save yourself, is a, natural, awareness. An, unlearned, understanding of what's required for your, internal, ease. So, stay conscious of where it comes from. And the purpose for its showing. To, always, be able to comprehend how, naturally, vital self-preservation must be to you. You should, also, come to trust God's presence residing in you and your sanctuary.

God's guard, is the force we'd, usually, tend to overlook. An innately rooted birth right, we must keep reminding ourselves to use. To remember, is to have a, good, relationship with that power. Whether you can acknowledge or ignore it? It is there, on time. All the time. So much so, any one of your protective mechanisms may appear, moments before the 'conscious' you could even respond. And is an enlightenment deserving of, daily, doses of grateful recognition. Because, every day, the security services of your system will, automatically, kick in to perform its works. Whether you were aware of its ignition or not? From blinking, crying, sneezing, and sweating. To the uncontrollable, unforced, snitching of your facial expressions, whenever there's some bullshit around.

We are equipped with a gang of miraculous sensors, gauges, and monitors. They alert our senses to whatever 'ain't cool' ass happenings, going on around us. But because it seems like ain't shit 'cool,' an expectancy for the interruption of stupidity is formed. Around the same time, this paranoia is produced, comes, another, reason to be angry. Funny, how that works, huh? And then, too often, the bullshit comes from the, emotionally, illogical minds, ways, and mouthpieces of the closest ones to us. We have given them pardons;

they've never begged for. Though, they've, surely, trespassed against us. I believe this is, also, a type of protecting yourself. It is, kind of, passive. But you are, still, dodging the aching pains of a loss. Being that they could be or were our loved one.

Most times, if we'd receive a hint of 'good looking out' from our folks, it is an afterthought of a reminder. Made only when the damage had, already, been done. Don't get me wrong. I mean, to get looked out for, at all, is good. But wake my game up before I take a hit, loss or beating. If only more foresight were used, in this life. We would do a better job of looking out for one another. Not, only, would messes become more avoidable. But your time could be saved and used a bit wiser. If your internal fight resembles a boxing match? Then, ducking, bobbing, and weaving mental and emotional punches, (your respect for) timing and reserving energy are perfect skills to possess. You, as the ref and both fighters, know all the rules to announce, before the first haymaker gets thrown. Meaning, in a you verse you? And it's called by you? How do you lose in an environment, like this? The answer is, YOU Don't! Because you should not. Especially, when your lesson(s) were learned. Still, an organized contest between two aggressors, don't got shit on the internal battles with oneself.

Whether the bout is sponsored by an outside instigator? Or it's an in-house, self-production? The fight is on. And will continue. In our confrontations, with self, the ability to be fair to you is, heavily, needed. Because when you're so invested or that close to it, you may not see how you can win. Or when you are winning. You can't even recognize the ways and the how, you are, presently, a success story. How's that? Well, just by wanting better for you. So that the best in you may prevail. It will. By accepting the challenges, you give yourself. And really seeing you are prepared and ready to throw down. Whenever the time comes. The squabbles, within you, put you in a weird but great position. Because the better in you, is looking at the best choices to make. For your sustainability. With the more ignorant side of you wanting the easiest way out or through. Which is, always, more trouble than it's worth. Due to the fact that, 9 out of 10 times, it's a, very, temporary fix. Therefore, the easiest way out, ain't the best way through.

Once you've fought, yourself, back to one peace, realize something, please? Only you can whoop you. Only you know how to beat you. Don't turn on yourself. Don't turn away from yourself. Push through. Goodness is, always, on the other side. Push. Because the God in you cannot hurt you. Nor does the, real, you in you, want to hurt you. Remember how you broke through, before, pretty much, unscathed? Hit, only, by a tough ass lesson to recall, to reapply. So, push. Continuing to push your life forward is the, greatest, way to protect you. From how you live and love. To how you make your money. Push. Push to prove a point to yourself.

And fuck what 'they' are talking about. Show you your worth. It's how you can win your life back. Anytime you look, inside your own head or heart, you may find some unlikable shit. The key is, for you not to be afraid to look. Reason being, by seeing your blemishes gives you the power to know what to fix, adjust or destroy. On top of that, the inspection grants a higher vantage point, for countering outside threats. The bad day, somebody else is having, can rain its, ugly, potential over your joy. Use your umbrella of compassion and kindness for you. Then you can extend a notion of 'safe space' to the rain maker. Knowing where you stand, with you, makes 'your' protection, work for everybody. Your, positive position, will help to eliminate the negative impact of outside factors. Their misunderstandings and disagreements. Which, ultimately, takes away the committal of unintentional offenses. And the lines of communication are open or extended, to all the information you can use.

One of the hardest things, in life, is dealing with the, real, stresses of yo shit. Plus, taking on the pressures of an overvalued, superficial relationship, at the same time. It can be, very, overwhelming. Taking care of yourself, includes who you choose to allow around you. Your circle has the power of influence. So, your best assessments are needed if you guys are like-minded. Even, if you are opposite thinkers with a well revered friendship. Your best assessment is as important. Assuming like-minds aren't, collectively, on some bullshit. As buds, together, good decisions are being made. Don't get shit confused, though. Opposite doesn't mean wrong or anything negative. But for the sake of a point. Let's say those thinking dissimilar to you 'are' on a bogus hype. Does being cool with them type of mothafuckas short circuit your aptitudes as an individual? Does it erase your ability to use your better judgement? Or are you in such a fucking, blind desperation to be accepted, you can't see how, way far left, you're playing yourself? That's some punk shit. And far removed from protection. To me, it is protection's antipodes. A contrarian idealism.

And a, blatant, assault of an inside job. Being carried out by, you, the captain of the vessel.

From being honest, with yourself, about your own issue(s) and your best, solid, viable solution(s). To understanding when to involve a coach or trainer, for more help. You are, ultimately, in charge of deciding who and what, will aid in achieving your life's goal(s). That help can come from any source, you trust. So, why not, first, trust your fucking self? You must know who, what and how you are, to do this. And God will, also, speak to and use you to be the example to you and to others. Walking with this light blesses you with foresight. Allowing you to make calm and clear choices. By looking inside, you, helps you to see you, out. Go. Control the narratives of your own life's outcomes. Be the reason for great results.

A Gangster's Guide To The 10 Rules To This Game
By Terrance Hutson
Do Unto Others

Even though, I am numbering these rules, there's no real, order of the other nine. These rules are not being lined out by level of importance. So, let's have less concern for the arrangement of placement. Shall we? Instead, let us focus on the order, that may be restored in your life, by understanding and applying, your own combo of precepts. Treating folks with kindness and respect could, arguably, sit at the top of your list of principles. It is, just as, valuable as any other 'self-set' mandate. "Do unto others as you would have them do unto you." Reads and sounds simple enough, right? It is, probably, the most, easily, understood and most recalled ordinance, ever. Which means, this chapter doesn't have to become a long and dragged-out point.

We've read versions of the phrase inside spiritual teachings. We have been told and taught this phrase, at, very, early ages. And each of these rules are relative or, strongly associated. I can see, 'do onto others...,' belonging to the self-preservation side of the game. However, it stands alone. And could have its own list of subcategories. Like, 'giving what you expect' and 'violence begets violence', for examples. What is so dope about this, specific, rule is its, obvious, point. Treat mothafuckas like you want to be treated. Easy as that. No haggling. There is no reason to look over the, vivid, intentions of such a credo. Having given consideration towards the manner you think you should be handled and talked to. Or loved. Or understood. It behooves you to behave from the perspective of kindness and respect. With yourself and especially, when dealing with others. Missing the basic logic of this principle can result in unfavorable returns, for you. Just by, you, Not returning the favor(s) of goodness brought to you. So, put in what you want to get back. You don't have to be hella philosophical or dumb ass religious, to see why and how, to practice these practices. Nor do you need hella book smarts to wrap yo mind around how much intelligence exists in living this rule.

'Doing unto others', may even be the most, plainly, realized statement, out of all of the rules. The absence of obscurities, in it, gives you a distinct grasping of the concept. Because it shows that you know how to be around and interact with people. And their reactions to your interactions, speak to your appropriateness. I have a little phrase I use. "I am in all ways, always appropriate." I use it as an affirmation, as a confirmation and a self-checking type of reinforcement. To help me continue to perform a, steady, maintenance of this rule. Which is why I could never understand how hate driven; humans can be. It is a fact that I don't like hella shit. From silly mothafuckas choices. Y'all end up crying over. When you knew it was a foul ass thought, in the first place. Let alone the following through with the foul. To y'all fucking selfishness. Or y'all numbness, blindness, and carelessness. To the lack of respect, you bitches show your fellow human. I've seen you, pieces of shit, hold more regard for animals, you'll never, fucking see, in real life. Than to, kindhearted, real live humans, that you look dead at, every fucking day. And these same fucks, have the nerve to judge the actions of the next man. It's, sadly, baffling. But what if each of us adopted another person to 'do unto'? Are you able to picture it? I am. And I have lived, as a silent component in helping people, for decades. Not just my own. But our people.

To love as you wish to be loved. To teach, to learn, too. To show up as a blessing is a blessing. Doing unto others is a, complete, win. And my skanless ass, almost, went as far as applying it to the negative side of the game, too. I mean if somebody is being fucked up towards me. My first mind would, most likely, be on some 'let me get the fuck from 'round' them. But what would linger, is my West West ass mind state of get back, retaliation and revenge. Word to Daz Dilli. Then, my self-checking would kick in. And I would begin to contemplate the benefits. And if there are any? What are they? Now, I have saved a life, energy, and a headache. All due to the consciousness of a trusted belief in, "Do Unto others as you would have them do unto you."

A Gangster's Guide To The 10 Rules To This Game

By Terrance Hutson

Keep Quiet

'You have the right to remain, the fuck, silent. What YOU say, Can and Will be used against yo stupid ass, in a court of laws that, still, don't got shit to do with you. You got the right to an attorney that is in cahoots with the judges, in a system of injustice and racial divides.' Fuck 'em! And you, shut the fuck up! Flat out. Make them hoes do they job. Being punk police is the only career where another mothafucka does the work for them. No investigation. No need in getting another agency involved. All the PD needs is lame ass fake tough guys. Like those Italian tellers out on the east coast. Or suckas mothafuckas like, 'to-catchie'(tekashi). Making them more famous, as targets. And confidential informants, that get mistreated, by a dickhead cop, for their help. Hella scary ass niggas telling, and shit is what should be criminal. With hood charges to face. Being convicted here, you will be "rehabilitated." Or "isolated." In most cases, the rat will not get a lesser sentence or financial compensation. Instead, they should be labeled, targeted, killed or in the best-case scenario, run they punk ass out the fucking neighborhood. Shut yo hoe ass the hell up.

This, tactical, verbal suppression is important because your life could depend on it. These days, it has become a thing where the victim calling the law, winds up dead. Where a typical, white bitch (Karen or Ken) contacts the punk police for nothing more than us 'livin' while Black'. And then he is murdered. Or there is shit planted, for false charges. So. Yeah. Fuck tha police! Their origins. And the clowns that keep informing they bitch ass. It does not take delving hella deep into, "I ain't saying shit because I ain't seen shit or heard shit." I have been, illegally, questioned and interrogated in that room, behind the apartments and in, little, dark ass alleyways. I ain't say shit, then and ain't gonna say shit, now. Offering information on anything other than your, specific, role is worthy of a checking, at the minimum. Disciplinary actions must be carried out, though. I am a firm believer in a few things. 1. One must have and adhere to some guidelines. 2. One must face consequences for their, good or bad, actions. 3. Everybody has a job to do. 4. If you cannot do that job? Then walk the fuck away and keep the fuck quiet. Why would you speak on somebody's name, business, relationship, or crimes? Whether you are speaking down or up. It doesn't seem natural. Are you that incomplete? Internally? How do you live with yourself? What do you see in the mirror? Can you stand to look? You'd better answer them honestly, too. Even if, we are in, direct, competition. Telling on a nigga, doing the same shit I am doing, can't happen, captain.

Snitching is snitching. Let them crime fighters do they job. This is, strictly, for mothafuckas involved in street laws and G codes. My Mom can tell on you niggas and not be held to street/snitch standards. Because she ain't in them streets. They 'might' have tried to fuck with me, for it. But, highly, doubtful. Because I told them, mothafuckas, once. Do not do yo hot shit between here and here. I will send yo ass there or there. And 'there,' is where you will be. Fuck with the game if you want to. Any who. Speaking outta turn, especially, when no one's asking you, has inescapable backlash tied to it. No matter the environment, there will, always, be a consequence to the notion of, 'speaking when not being spoken to.' Because not everything you see or hear should be told. I am not, just, talking about snitch shit. Apply it where and when you deem it necessary. At home with your lover. On the job. Or outside, anywhere. Keeping shit to yourself could be the difference between, getting that shit put in yo life. And you making it home, to school, work, or church. It can make the deciding call to your new beginning or a sad ending. Minding your own business, saves lives. Yes, speaking on it does, too. When your, 'civilian,' eyes have witnessed some bullshit. At this point, it is an intervention or rescue mission. Not telling. When you are helping another person from being hurt, or worst. You should not feel or think you have done something wrong, for doing a good thing. Turning a blind eye, should, make you a guilty party. Punk police. Um. Hello. You bitches in blue say citizens need to say something if they see something. But y'all mouths and eyes don't work. Shit. Tell on yo niggas, police. I am going to prison if I was in the car, with a nigga who, just, killed somebody. You should, too. And I would probably, acquire more charges for not telling. As if the law/society hold its, regular, citizens to a higher standard than the lawmakers, law enforcers, the government, presidents, and preachers. But the pawn police are exempt from regulations and consequences? How? Because they are special? Fuck no. But because they are expendable. The front-line crash test dummies, for a nation that is losing its grip. The pawn police fall for the false sense of purpose. Making them dumb enough to think they are important. It will be too late when silly ass oinks will, be the squealing, dying strategic diversion. While their superiors are sucking dicks and kissing asses to get a seat, in a vehicle that will not ever stop for the help. Facts. Fucking servants. The pawns living in the cities they are to serve, have a better chance to bridge the gap between their neighbors and their coworkers.

Making it can, also, depend on what you are saying and if you're saying too much. Showing concern and being in somebody's business, is a tossup to perception. And a thin line, indeed. Choosing words wisely or 'watching your mouth' keeps you from having to watch yo back. Maintain an awareness of how quickly words can turn a cordial interaction into total carnage. Ask any nation about it. You cannot be shocked by their answers. Wars have been fought. Lives lost. And countries destroyed because of words. Some battles, in our little worlds, start due to this same type of shit. "Wars of words," will continue to thrive, when there is an absence of logic, respect, and honor. The noticeable respect shown by an attentive listener, lends a hand of opportunity for the speaker to, also, grant such graces. Now, an actual, helpful communication is taking place. All from speaking out of helping intentions. Also, by a display of patience and reverence, as the hearer and the bearer.

For me, it boils down to a, simple, education. Just be yo ass the fuck quiet. Often, being quiet and still allows you to receive information clearer. Processing the info becomes, that much, easier. Fun fact. Silent and listen share the same letters. Let that marinate. And by combining the two, a borderline superpower has been found, in you. As that soaks in. Realize how much is taught and learned, in this condition. From the inner settings of your desire, wanting and giving understanding. To the completely, applicable sense it makes, logically. Shedding, more, light on phrases like, "the loudest one, is the weakest link." And this one, "the squeakiest wheel, needs the oil." Here is one of my favorites, though, "Before you mind my business, mind yours." It reads and sounds clear as fuck. Minding your own business, in hella ways, shows how important you are to you. One. It is self-preservation at its finest. And how you mind your business, serves as a window's peek into your character. As far as trust and respectability goes.

I heard somebody say, "more actions and less announcements." That is, some of, the most solid shit I've heard in a minute. It speaks, distinctly, to this chapter's topic of, keeping quiet. We talk too much. I am guilty. Which translates into how I could not have been listening. Because I was making announcements. A while ago, I had noticed a cold ass, pattern occurring. It would take place, shortly, after I opened my mouth. I was minding my business. But I kept exposing my hand and plans, to mothafuckas who, one, did not care, at all. And two, could give a fuck less about my announcements. Nope. It is not the same thing. The they, 'didn't care at all,' part is that folks got they own shit to do and think about. 'Give a fuck less,' speaks to the lack of importance my announcements held, with others. Anyway. I've seen friends move faster, than I could, on my ideas, I disclosed in trust. If they cannot be considered stolen? Then, I had turned them over, willfully. I've had, other, unassuming shares get riddled with, negativity and dubious jokes. But the thing that I had the hardest time grasping, was the why? I would speak on the possibilities in front of me, but they would disappear. I don't know, what? But there was something snatching my blessings, right from my possession and vision. I blamed the punk ass devil, at first. I, quickly, realized that that bitch ain't got power, over me, like that. Nor do the bitch got, any, authority in my life. It had to be a lesson lesson in it, for me. Live from my source of peace. And a lesson, indeed. I've learned that the energy wasted on impure focuses will never yield good fruit. What impurities? You might ask. Shit like, announcing anything for an envious reaction or to get under someone's skin. Or if it's coming from any angle of deception and bullshit? You should, no longer, be able to see it. Let alone to receive the blessing, anymore. Use more energy and control to finish the tasks you, may, want to announce. Then broadcast it. Can't shit get in the way of it or stop it, now.

A Gangster's Guide To The 10 Rules To This Game

By Terrance Hutson

Play It How You Say It

Play it how you say it. Walk it like you talk it. And my, very own, personal favorite, "if I told you, I showed you." My actions have, always, matched my words. There may be someone, out there, who can say, 'nah, not always.' But I've been so solid, for so long, I cannot recall any instances. Nor the hater that might say it. However, I can recollect the first time I learned the severity of poor decision making. Beginning back in my, dirty, West Oakland nigga days. My young crew, we were for real about our hustle. Each one of us had real life responsibilities. As 11- and 14-year-old kids. From paying rent, bills to groceries and school shit. Our need to hustle and how we did it, caught the interest of our elders in the game. One of the OGs, took me under his wing. And I remember when he chose me to go on a ride with him. I did. We drove the short distance to another side of Oakland. On the drive, I was informed that we were on our way to collect a debt. We get there and the mothafucka ain't got the money, of course. So, of course, disciplinary actions got taken. And as we are leaving, my OG says, 'if you gon be about this hot shit? You better stand on y'all agreement." He goes on to, almost, explain the missing pieces of his statement. As to make sure I, fully, get what needs to be learned, here. He says, "that nigga should've walked it, like he talked it. That fake ass nigga was 'posed to keep it a thou wow. And play it how he say it. Not, out here, having niggas trippin' 'bout they chips." Then he told me, "nephew, This shit, basically, just 'grown folks' shit'."

When you create an image, but you are not a paid actor, you are putting you at risk. Don't break character. The impersonations don't impress anybody. You will either come off like a clown, doing too much. Or you'll get recognized for your, fake ass, persona. And cut off or in pieces. But in this climate of clout chasers, body augmentations and getting famous for nothing, what's real? Besides the blindness? The numbness? What gets offered as answers, is more upsetting than the living lie. We've made false narratives more attractive than the truth. But is the truth that ugly, though? Not to me. I will stare her ugly ass dead in the fucking face and tongue the ugly ass, true bitch down. Before I'd start to try to listen to a beautiful ass lie.

Society and technology perpetuate the normalcy of fraudulent activities. From America letting the Weinstein brothers get away with their criminal acts. To the 45th orange thief of state's history of felonies and treason. To the discovery of tons of untalented, overnight stars. We have let TV, the news, and social media cloud our minds, with bullshit. And we are using the fucking internet to make up our lives, now. Because somehow, everybody, on like shit. Between exposes, posts, memes, emojis and hella platforms to click on. You can have the 'tea' to spill, on any celebrity and get an invite to a show or podcast. Becoming famous. Or do the dumbest shit, in life. Just to find your ignorance has secured sponsorship. For nothing. You can start or follow a trend and go viral. Generating another source of income, in days. I mean, hit the lick. Get yo paper. But stay down until you come up. Some of us are blessed with talents. A small percentage, of the group, has gotten lucky enough to be in the right place at the right time. Contrarily, most people must work, extra, hard just to get by. A fraction of this group will dedicate their focuses to their gift. They love doing it. Practice it. Perfect it. And still, might not make a fucking dime from it. But happy happy. Because there is no pretending. Living in your truth will help you play it, how you say it.

Unfollow or block that, goofy ass internet, way of thinking. Are views and likes, really, that important, to you? If it's not for business networking? Finding and/or chatting with family and old friends? What's the point? Setting out to impress a virtual society? Is this when the pretending begins? Now, that could be strategic. You might be inclined to embellish your posts, a bit. To attract more clicks. But does that qualify as false advertising? Your life's story might be, quite, interesting. Or not even. Just let it reflect the truth. I mean, do your thing. Let a, real, focus make some loot for you. Not revealed lies making a fool out of you. Like I let that notification bell feature make out of me. I felt like a trained animal by my reactions to hearing, ding. Only to realize the alert was for someone I follow but not an actual friend. The warning was set so I didn't miss anything. To wind up a little pissed. Because I am notified, regularly, about some bullshit. Not a job lead or contracting opportunity. Nope. But some person, whom I don't know, puts in different color contact lenses in each eye. And that shit is fucking trending.

But like any other noise, I'm going to check it out. Even if I was in the middle of something else. I am going towards the noise. What's so, very, obvious here? Obviously, I'm not able to do or finish my thing when I'm doing some other shit. This makes me a dildo. A fake fuck. On me. Because I put this other shit, before my shit. The whole while, wondering why it feels like I hadn't made, any, progress? And haven't. All because of the way we can get in our own way. Some of us aren't, even, used to quiet and calm. It seems, we have been addicted to chaos. As if, the drama is making our environments normal to us. Why, though? Are we, all, histrionic? Thirsty for attention? Or narcissists? High for the attention we give ourselves. It comes from a training to be okay with being in, around or a part of drama. The being okay with it is formed in the confusion of calamity. Or in the bowels of the hearts and minds of a shitty society. Where the plot to take advantage of you or a situation fester. Giving the people, you allow in, notions to keep trespassing. Their encroachment is the byproduct of not establishing, clear, boundaries. But since you are as passive as the rest, you get taken. Then taken, again. All the while, watching thieves tiptoe off with your blessings. Under the cover of your own consent. One more time. Be clear about your stance, intent, and unease. It can lessen how often you are in, around and a part of dumb shit.

Words mean something, even, unsaid. So, once they are spoken, these words have a life. Now, they are your words, living in dual action. You're talking. With them hearing. And like human life, a living word is powerful and feeble, at the same time. As soon as you start lying, you and your comments, turn weak as fuck. You can't be trusted. Which boils down to you being an unreliable switcher. Which is bad for business. In the Town if that reputation precedes you? You should move. Who wants to be known as a fibbing fuck? I've seen niggas spew out fake ass personals, false ass testimonies and bogus ass hater statements to females, just for some pussy. So ain't no telling what hoe ass niggas is doing for some bread. Okay. I have lied TO some pussy. But not FOR some pussy. I have lied to the punk police, in court and to my lady, before. Though, I can validate my doing it. I felt guilty. Mentally, I didn't give a fuck. But in my soul, there was contrition. I didn't regret lying to any of them. I wasn't tripping off that. My spirit felt sorry, for me. Not from pity. But from its foresight into the, lonely, travels of a scary ass lying piece of shit. To save me from the inside, out. Freedoms are granted for standing in/on your truth. Me living, fairly, fabrications free, I've seen, positive, returns on the patience and intent, I've invested.

Adding peace to my character. And positive, deposits of belief, on my account. Which strengthens the spirit and the ability, for others, to rely on my word. Because honestly, there are no, real, reasons to lie.

A Gangster's Guide To The 10 Rules To This Game

By Terrance Hutson

Bomb First

I, probably, should've put this rule with protecting yourself. Apparently, I didn't. I could have. In the aspect of physically defending yourself. This is an excellent rule. At some point or another, in life, we have all had to throw them hands. We've put 'em up with siblings, cousins, friends and the occasional stranger. Anybody on any list can get minked up. Speaking of lists and anybody getting elected to the minks. How did 'the minked' run their campaign? Emotionally? And not logically? What was the deciding vote? Was it under their noses? Yep! Sure, the fuck was under the nose! Yo fucking mouth! It is always their fucking mouths. That's what happens to y'all asses all the damn time. You hoe ass clowns get too emotional and go to bumping ya yaps. Not thinking. Just barking hella snarky like, though. Now here come the minks. Mink, mink, mink. Mink.

I believe more folks should receive a good ass whooping, from time to time. Because the lesson that needed to be taught. At home. By loved ones. Was, either, never understood or studied. Or was never their resident's curriculum. Now, outside is educating the shit out of you. And how you've avoided death, thus far? Is dumb ass baffling, to me. Folks have become murder victims for way less. Or were never found. Due to behavior such as yours. Even with bombing first, the quality of your character shows. Did you sucker-punch the opp? Was the offender expressing apologies, regret or how it is a simple misunderstanding? Could you have walked away? Were you on your gentleman or lady shit? Or were you on yo overreacting, fuck boy hype, to a nothing ass situation? So, yeah, either way. Both the offender and defender, still, have a responsibility to each other, logic, and intention.

Again, every ass might need to or should get touched on. Just so folks may keep believing, with reminders readily available. Of why there shall be repercussions. Whether yo punk ass was aware of yo mistakes or not. Which is, most likely, the reason behind your two pieces. No biscuit. In our culture, the 'biscuit' is a euphemism for a pistol. When pistol play is involved, shit becomes a different ballgame. Use your forethought/foresight, prior to taking things to the extremes of upping pipes for pole dancing. Escalating to this type of violence carries its own set of follow-up results. From dying in the streets. To life on a yard. From having to watch yo back, all the damn time. To the jeopardy your family members are now in. The misgoverning of your anger and behavior poses a threat to your world. And trust me, it ain't as easy to make it out as you might imagine. It's scary as hell. You don't know how it ends. Or when? Who's all involved? Every unfamiliar face looks like some bullshit needs to be knocked off it. Or they look like a snitch. I'm sure, a high percentage of society ain't cutthroat like that. They don't want smoke like that. They are not popping shit out or off. Which is great. But some is.

'Bombing first,' explains itself. If it's up? Then, it's stuck. And I'm getting off. First. And last. Just as this law is related to protection. It ties in with 'play it how you say it', also. However, I felt it should get a little recognition, as a standalone topic. I won't take too long on it. But I do want to add a slight twist to it. Follow me. Imagine your first reaction being a solution. Not panic or anxiousness. Not reacting out of, sudden, direst or confusion. Just an immediate reply that you see yourself using. Now, remember you are 'reacting'. Because of something that happened, beforehand, for you to respond to. Stimulating an initial retort to solve the problem(s). You didn't run, fold, or give in to the pressure. You saw the issue(s), as they appeared. Pulled the trigger on a choice. Then pushed a hard line, trying to make it work in your favor. Lead with this different kind of 'bomb first' methodology. For you, in this life. As a, fairly, responsible person, looking for answers to life's tests will result in your peace of mind. And you owe some peace to yourself. It is hella hard out here, already. Don't let the fear to choose wind up picking a route for you. Maintain control. By choosing the remedy that works best for you, first. Finding a fix, from jump, allows room for a head bumping or two. This can be expected, right before you have things, completely, figured out. But you've given yourself a head start, by identifying the obstacle(s). And you concluding a cure to stop the potential hindrance.

As I mentioned, previously, 'bomb first' is connected to the 'Protect yoself at all times' rule. To me, one's ability to protect themselves depends on their choice making strengths. Sometimes, we, truly, may not have a clue as to what to do next? Sometimes, we get overwhelmed. We get tired of being sick and tired. We are weary, fragile, and afraid, at times. But we cannot quit. No tapping out. And the fact of knowing you cannot forfeit, no show or call in a sub, Low-key, gives you the upper hand. How? Simple. Wrapping your mind around what can't take place, places you in a starting position. You may not be able to tell folks what will happen. But you're able to say what ain't. So, here, an automatic choosing has commenced. And to me, you have just unconsciously bombed first. From there, since surrendering is not an option, you can use your energy to solve shit.

The link that getting off first attaches to 'play it how you say it', often, leads to verbal conflicts or violent ones. But bound, nonetheless. Let me land, right quick. If you say you will but don't, at this point, you've initiated a conflict. Conflict to words. Words to being bomb on, first. So, be about it! Or do without it!

A Gangster's Guide To The 10 Rules To This Game

By Terrance Hutson

Each 1, Reach 1, Teach 1

I live by this mothafucka, here. Man, I mean that! Ask about me? I am the quintessence of the rule. I, genuinely, want everybody to be okay, think okay and do okay. To the extreme where if I hear or see that you're not, I will do my best to make it better. Some way. Whether it's some help in action. Or with, seemingly, perfect word choices. Or by being there and listening. I am capable of being appropriate, in all ways, always. I promote others to do something similar. I reinforce positivity. I have discernment. The energies of this life have found me useful. They and I are integrated. I can't ignore nor will I squander my gifts. And the only judgement I carry out is in two parts. First. I will, certainly, determine the worth of the situation. It all depends. But there are levels here, too, for me. One. Do I mention it to the judged, extending them a chance to correct their course? Two. Do I check them hella hard? Or do I leave? Choices shepherd possibilities. My discernment lives actuated. It stays up and on go. Plus, the use of foresight takes the lead, no matter what. As the proper preparation to a choice.

Having qualities like these, is what qualifies me as a great teacher. Knowing this, adds power to my willingness to reach anybody, anywhere. That power is noticeable. It has a pull. I've been in possession of it for a long ass time. People of all ages, backgrounds, gangs, churches, and genders seemed to have been drawn to me. I would be minding my own business. And BOOM! Out of nowhere, a stranger comes up to me and shares their whole life. I have laughed so hard with, total, strangers. I have wept in, true, sadness. Next to someone I'd met 14 minutes prior. And upon leaving me, they are compelled to tell me, "Hey brother, I love you." "I love you, back," is my, automatic, return.

I am going to tell you guys a story, right quick. A few years ago, I went to Jacksonville, Fl. I was introduced to a bunch of wonderful folks, affiliated with this one family. It was the beginning of summer. There were relatives, in this family, graduating from high school and college. Some were headed to the military. And the parents of these kids, anniversary was this weekend. Hella shit was going on. I was there for it. As I entered their home, through a side door as directed, I locked eyes with an older lady. She had to be well in her 80s. She was on a motorized scooter. Wearing a night gown and a house coat. I am, barely, over the threshold to this lovely home. When we just started smiling big stupid ass smiles, at each other. Mind you, the whole time, her, and I never lose eye contact. I know the person that invited me was trying to do the formalities. But I, 'Spike Lee movie,' glided over to her. Gliding. No steps taken. Just a, big ass, hug, and kisses on my face. Then I took a seat, next to her. And with no words, we smiled, uncontrollably, together. I felt like I missed her. But we just met. Then she spoke on something our spirits were aware of, right away. She said, "baby, please don't think I'm loony? And I know I don't know you. But I do. I know you from another life." And without missing a beat, I told her that I knew her, as well. Not on no funny shit, though. I, really, believed our loves were, very, familiar with one another. A love that comes from a, not too far-fetched, dimension of now and then. One of us crossed over. I think it was me.

    Me and my new friend from the past, sat there and talked, like we had old times to catch up on. I won't go into the details of our powwow. But she did give me gems, a light, and some messages. She told me to embrace these spiritual attractions. They may be more drawn to me. But some will pull you nearer.

Either way, I must look beyond sight to be of service. I hadn't stopped, since. She went on to tell me that I am one of the ones who can help them. Who is them? Help how? Were never my questions. If I had? It would've been, why me? I knew the answer to that, though. I didn't have any questions. I understood her meaning with my entire self. From my core to my shell, I knew. My God and Universe guided us here. I was supposed to be right there, right then. I was close to her through the source of life and the light. I will never lose or forget the power I witnessed that evening. She changed my life, forever.

 I saw the term 'kindred spirits' evolve into the closest thing to proof of natural miracles. I felt, exactly, what the word Love was created from. In that instant, something in my system stimulated, what can only be described as advanced sensory development. I was now the host for some super sensitive energies. Basically, no one is alien, to me. I know you. And way more than you can fathom. All I need to do is be within 4-5 feet of you. I can feel who you are. Give me a few words of conversation, only seconds, and I will tell you, HOW you are? Hang out, with me, for a while and you will know, WHY you are this? To me, we are not strangers. HERE'S A CHALLENGE. TRY ME! CONTACT ME! TEST

ME ON WHAT I SAID! If you are not convinced, I will give your money back. For the counselling session and this book. I'm not trying to cajole you into anything. I am nowhere near religious. I, truly, just know, love, and trust the origins of this, amazing, gift. That is mine. I am favored. It sounds like I'm talking high powered. I am. Because it is 'High power'. Having been blessed in such a manner, I must use it for, all, its intents, and purposes. Whether that is helping, leading, guiding, reminding, finding, coaching, or counselling. Feeding, protecting, honoring, or respecting. I am made to reach and teach. It is my pleasure. And job.

A Gangster's Guide To The 10 Rules To This Game

By Terrance Hutson

Don't Shit Where You Eat

At one point, I didn't know how this rule made me hella disrespectful, to my Mom. Not, only, was I sneaking to do the shit. I put our whole household in jeopardy. For a fonky ass 6, $700 a week. But also, Moms mentioned the rule. Specifically, to me. And I, still, chose to be shitty. I was fake uncivilized. Until I got caught up doing some other shit that landed me in 150th. CYA. The California Youth Authority. Where I met a guy, who gave me game on how it goes. What to do and not to do. He said this was his 3rd time here. When he hits 18, he is serving the rest of a 35yr sentence in prison. This made him realize his, avoidable, mistakes. One was, the fact, none of the money, risks, or bonds, we think we have, were worth losing his kids. Nor his family and real friends or his freedom. He talked like an older man, at 17. He said, now he has a deeper, better appreciation for parents. His Dad turned him in. Sounds fucked up, don't it? Yes. But not really. His folks told him the same as mines. Don't shit where you eat.

As a grown ass man, not into a bunch of the hot shit, all like that. I can say with knowing and understanding this rule, it has carried me further in this life than imaginable. Seeing the sense to apply, not shitting where you eat, kept me out of skanless scenarios many of my peers had to endure. I ain't with it. I need to be overlooked when it comes to the delivery of y'all hoe shit. I have developed a whole way behind my logic. Do you know how much bullshit gets missed from being made like this? Do you know many lives I've saved by mothafuckas not knowing where I lived, when I was wiggling? Or my routes? How much 'fonk' I avoided, just by me, doing my dirty shit, away from my zone? If I would have stepped on known toes, I would've been foul or out of pocket. And that puts somebody in a position of retaliation. With the drop on me. So, to me, when you install a process for this ruling. You give yourself the advantage of more peace of mind. Unless you'd rather have a piece of mind? If so? Put this mothafucka down and don't read no more of my books! Nah. Matter fact. You need these series of services the fucking most. Keep yo eyes on the page. Any fucking way. Doing your shitty shit around your living spaces, is not of protection. Hell. Even being shitty, shows how much you are not of a protective mind. You are, totally, destructive. As fuck.

Hella, hexxa, extra destructive. To yo own self person. Let alone the people, you say, you care about. This, too, is an example of taking a dookie in the dwelling, you feed. Your body holds a spirit. This spirit holds a connection to the energies of life. This connection, to this life, holds the responsibility of construction or reconstruction. Build your spirit up from the rumble of, what might be, reality, now. Add some Crossbeams if you see fit. Amen. Learn and find yourself. Give of yourself. There are so many things you can do to improve the area(s) of your life that needs a fix. It starts by enhancing your thinking. Any other take is, you, shitting on the table of yo soul. Ugh. That image, alone, should force you to turn away from such a disgusting offense.

If you thought hard enough? You would find the mental ability to include infidelity. That's in the physical, emotional, and financial realms of cheating. It can, all, begin and remain great. Or end, terribly, with your choices. To not want to bring harm, is a lover's choice. To never mind the harm to come, is a piece of shit. Where you eat. But will have the nerve to apologize. Mostly, it is because they punk ass got caught. Like high 90s, in percentages. Be the person who is good with being good. And doing good by others. There's no need to complicate the truth. You wanna go do something else? Say that. If what you have is the best thing you ever experienced? Live that! Don't let the facts scare you. Facts or the truth are, both, there and available so, you can make perfect choices. The information at hand, grants the opportunity for clarity. Clarity, aids in good choice making. Good choice making, create better people. And lives.

A Gangster's Guide To The 10 Rules To This Game
By Terrance Hutson
Anything's Possible, Nothing's Fasho

Each one of us got a story. Most of these stories start off hella grimy or gloomy. Filled with losses, fear, being broke and in danger. Sickness, sadness, savagery, and selfishness. Our, similar, tales are told through the eyes of our world. A world where tries, dreams and uncertainties produce cries and lies. Where promise and hope gets replaced with conform and racism. Where love became harder to see or join in its performances. And trust is, still, considered a myth of a hoax. Only to be witnessed and experienced by our elders or small children. Young men and women could, merely, wonder at the possibilities, of trust. But we have, all, come from beneath the trauma. The evil. The stress. Somehow. We keep making it through. So, everyday fight for your life. Everyday. Find for the shit that is worth it, to you. Fight to have it or keep it. Just do what you did to get there. You'll never know. You might destroy demons. You may locate yo groove thang. Or discover your missing peace. Because anything is possible, nothing is for sure.

Even though, right now, your life looks hella different from your yesteryear. You know what it took to arrive here. Always, make yourself recall it. Keep the folks who kept you focused. Continue to give them their flowers, too. None of us have or can make it, up, alone. Every one of us has, at least, one mothafucka that we are sure they rock with us, hella, strong. We, all, also, have somebody that we will kill a rock for and choke a tree over. It shall not be taken lightly. Because nothing is fasho. I have lost, so many, people over the last two years, it's ridiculous. Selfishly, I wish I could have them back. For just one more hug, convo, or something. I miss my Great Grandparents, on my Mom's side. And my Grandparents, on my Dad's side. So much. They loved so real. I didn't think they would or could, ever, leave me. The fact that I had a chance to be raised by them, helps me know, I will, always, have them, here. I got to learn good and simple lessons, sitting on those front porches. The teachings out of the mud, hit different. They stick to you. I have, definitely, seen, felt, and dealt with the deaths of others. Some of the losses, I, still, mourn over. I gain strength from remembering that love. Some, I think of and start smiling. I think my loved ones feel my energy when I'm reminiscing. And that is a joy to the core. Plus, I believe I've lived a life, with and around them, that they all knew we left off in a great place. Loving is possible.

Now, since, we know nothing is for sure. Don't fuck off your opportunities. From your good relationships. To your job/career. From speaking up and out. To helping out and picking somebody up. Any chance you get to be up or assist. Take it. Take it because you, genuinely, want to. Have true, genuine efforts because it may not be reciprocated. If you're doing it from the goodness of your heart? Without an injection of an agenda. You don't have expectations, all like that. Which, preserves you, your feelings, and the relationship. In turn, this make others see the appreciation you have for them. And you walk away with a healthier spirit, in position to continue to get blessed. Blessed af. Word to Ronnie Jordan. Knowing you're blessed is possible.

I have seen and been a part of some miraculous gifts, in this life. The birth of my children. The, rapid, healing of my son. The last few verdicts. I saw this Country stand on one accord. And change the rest of the World. One of these miracles changed my world, forever. Though, it is tied to a gang of pain and confusion. It was and is a gift, all the same. Back in 1996, my Mom was diagnosed with lupus. Several months later, we were told she didn't have much longer with us. Yet, the doctors had no basis or backing for their assessment. They were firm on her dying, soon. But it is 2021 and we, still, have our Mother. Lupus does come with a lot of body aches and deterioration. But I can call or go see her, today.

  Goodness is possible. The inspiration found in survival, can make the survivor and their witness, both, victors in, any, unfolding scenario. For those reasons, I am a victor. I know it with my, whole, heart. Honor in yo honesty gotta start living in our systems. Confessing an acknowledgement of where you've been or came up from, ain't shameful. Including where you are, right now. There is power in claiming it. That spark blazes to a fireball of self-gratification that's, unparalleled. Nothing matches you being on yo damn shit. Nothing. Then adding, the one witness or few, who will use your energy to see shit better. Or different? For themselves. Mothafucka, say what? I have been on both sides of the 'showing and seeing' spectrum. And I must say. Seeing, does something to the soul. It make you wanna show yo own ass. That's the shit. It help us, real niggas, keep believing in real shit. Like loving somebody or yoself enough to kill over. Fuck die for. Okay. Die for too. But nigga. Do something before yo fucking dying, though, first. Fuck! Fight back, bih! Damn it! Survival, possible.

Having an example or being the example are, equally, dope. The seeing and showing as survivor and witness shine, victoriously. But the same fact can, also, turn them into a victim. Somehow, we let our triumphs become our burdens. Whether it's survivor's remorse? Or the fear of winning. We put restrictions on what we are able to enjoy, for our own selves. As if, having a direction, executing the plan, and following through was a walk in the park. Like we shouldn't acknowledge the work it takes or took to reach these heights. Playing an active role in how and what things happen in your life, sends a message. Which, most often, translates into others caring, too. And giving a damn is, almost, free. It, only, costs the taking of action. Every able-bodied person has the same, yet, unique, responsibility to do something. Don't offer excuses. Just do work. Anytime you add actions to your passions, you've become a success. Because you have, literally, moved closer to the possible. Every little step you take forward, will attract your desires. The door to all things yours will open, for you. Truth is possible.

Random. Shout out to Pinky Black. A new platform. Bringing help with and awareness to the cancers in autochthonous American communities. We thank you. Their existence taught me, by doing my part, I have made a difference. This applies to each of us. I relish the idea of this union, actually, uniting. We have one common cause. Participating in the liberties of this life. And if we aren't the ones with little liberties? Then, we know them. We know what is holding them back or down. We know what we can do, if you were willing, to solve for why. All of us on our, one, accord. How would that look? Can you see peace spreading? I can. Every day, just step out on faith. To believe. Take the hand of another. To know you're not alone. Have a genuine respect for helping. To know joy. Gift your love. To accompany peace. And we will see, true, freedom is possible.

A Gangster's Guide To The 10 Rules To This Game
By Terrance Hutson

Any Is Plenty

Having any is better than not having shit, right? Yeah. Facts. The attention you mothafuckas pay to another mothafucka's bread, is a, damn, shame. Pocket watching is why you never find money in yours. Coveting? Jealousy? I'm not sure. Whatever it is, can't benefit you. In no way. There's a saying, 'what you eat don't make me shit'. I saw a double meaning in it. The first one is obvious. The other, I concluded. The '…don't make me shit,' part made me think about how much you do or have don't mean shit, to me. Because I beast out, too. And mines is plenty.

You don't, always, get what you deserve. But I do know you get what you've earned, worked for, or negotiated. Anything more, might come with another price. Follow me, right quick. In my head, the 'more' could be considered, your, blessing. But that blessing can, also, belong to somebody else. I mean, good things orbit. In the rotation, turns get missed. Staying in position to not be skipped, takes a choosy love. And now, with your wan to have 'more' you've taken it, just to have more. You're acting like a nigga who ain't ever had shit. Does that make sense? I get it. Fasho. Because I never had shit. But. Whoa. We quick to act like we shitless. We keep good shit to use. I ain't ever had shit, except, love, lessons, my name, my word, my solid, integrity, class, decorum and my mothafucking Blackness. All the parts of my life's necessary shit. From this, I am content. After that? Shit gets thrown in the game. To me, when I am satisfied, I am, more, able to enjoy seeing others get their piece. Mines will, always, replenish. Not all of us have faith like that. So, those of us who do? Our duty is to serve. With joy. To teach with inclusion. To share the things that will not come from anywhere else. To benefit in all of the ways you should. Why? Because anything is plenty, man.

A Gangster's Guide To The 10 Rules To This Game
By Terrance Hutson
My Brother's Keeper

Loyalty over money. Love over everything. Death before dishonor. Bros before hoes. I eat, we eat. All of these are sentiments of the rule. Being my brother's keeper is one of life's greatest and underrated responsibilities. Looking out for your fellow man, also, falls under the notion. In most cases, the deed is returned. I am fortunate, enough, to have a dope ass, younger Brother. And big Sis. Shout out to the Oracle. So, it wasn't hella hard to do my job. As keeper. Like I said. He dope. So, he has the ability to oversee, as well. Ask anybody. And they will tell you about the bond, these, two 'real' live mothafuckas got. You can say, "well, y'all 2 supposed to be tight. Y'all blood." Facts. We should be close. My, whole, family is. Yet, that ain't the story of, all, siblings. Or families, for that matter. I say it has, everything, to do with the individuals. If I was a hoe ass nigga? My brother, who isn't, would not fuck with me, in any way, flat out. None of my folks would. I am, very, thankful for the qualities possessed to have not been a witness of their disdain for sucka shit. Being solid keeps loyalty in its, proper, place.

Loyalty. What does that mean to you? Does the obligation become a burden? Or an honor? Can you remain loyal, in treachery? Are you, even, supposed to? To that? It is a fuck no, for me. To me, it is a badge of probity I wear, proudly. Simply because someone trusted, expected, and needed me to come through, that way. And I am, loyally, liable to oblige them, gratefully. I see the ability to be loyal as the difference between, knowing and not having a fucking clue. Clues about you and who you are. A clue into what a real, good, solid human looks like. Or should move like. Or can become. The big thing with loyalty is its natural existence, in us. If it isn't, innate? It is, still, normal, or automatic to pick a side and rock with it. From family ties. To the extended fam. From un and organized sports. To the homies and home-girls. Sides get chose. Who/what are you loyal to? Is your faithfulness respected. Does the devotion get shown back to you? The answers to these questions will, always, be 'yes' from the ones, truly, of your tribe.

Love over everything. Actually saying, place love over everything sounds like the easiest, toughest shit to do. Easy, when you are made of love. But tough for folks who hadn't known love's look. I thought it was impossible, for someone, to not know loving. Until I began to live this, little, life of mines. And seen it was fucked up outside. They, either, out here with, big, hatred. Or hatin'. They are killing relatives, for nothing. Backstabbing and biting. Lying. Cheating on love. Taking and stealing. Shit's crazy out there. Now, I know. No love, really, is possible. Fuck that! It is hella havable. You have it, already. Because you can tell you are not getting loved on. The love starts with you loving you, better. If you think I'm bullshitting? Try out what I'm saying. Consider yourself a tanch, more. Say where it hurt at. Tell the pain you got something for its punk ass. And love loving you love you. You will find that other people see, exactly, what you're doing. They will call it inspiration. We love being inspired.

    I didn't, always, have this approach. I, still, don't like shit. It's cool. Everybody know. Even Baby. Which is why I've taken a "Vow 2 Vibe." Something my lady and I came up with, Lovin' on one another. A commitment to making it make sense. Even in the times of selfishness. Come on, now. We, all, selfish, a little. If you're selfish and you know it, clap yo fucking hands. I just did. But we're not careless, though. There is a difference. Plus, caring for self is care. So, anyway. Take an oath. To your person and yourself to try clarity, first. Then when you face times of a letdown. You can express it. Without thinking about or causing an ending. In times of fear. Confess it. And include the 'why'? Practicing loving over everything, builds the connection of the union. Especially, in the tough and uncomfortable shit. You will see. How this 'special' treatment can change your life, in love. It works when all is good, too. At that, very, moment you notice you feel great. Or was told something hella cool. Or when you just caught yoself staring at that mothafucka. Speak on it. It'll make y'all feel sexy, as fuck. Vow 2 vibe. Keep at communicating clearly, intentionally, and openly. Make the promise to respect, y'all shit, enough, to show you do.

Now. Death before dishonor. "Bet I bomb on em first..." You got to be one of them ones for this part of the game. I mean. Shit. What I'm gonna say? You is. Or you ain't. For me, in this man shit, I have been solid. It ain't a dust speckle of smut on my name. I have and will remain a stand-up nigga. Hell. I'm standing, right now. I can say, wholeheartedly, I will kill something before I just die. But I'd rather die before I let, any, one of you mothafuckas make me into some shit I ain't. Straight the fuck up! I digress. Okay. Each of these rules are connected to the other. They relate because proper behavior, is a thing. They offer a way to believe and be. They give clues to how you can? Why you should? When to be that? And what, now or next? To be able to keep your brother (fellow man or woman) takes a keen sense of the rules. Knowing them helps you teach them. Seeing the reasons helps you show, there are reasons. Policies are in play to maintain order. You must supply yourself with order. The alternative is, literally, chaotic.

www.ingramcontent.com/pod-product-compliance
Lightning Source LLC
Chambersburg PA
CBHW070051200426
43193CB00054B/1764